STAY SAFE ONLINE

Learn Things About Fraud And Fraudsters

...An insider's Perspective

By

Franklin Ndubuisi Ahaotu

Copyright © 2021 Franklin Ndubuisi Ahaotu,

All rights reserved

Table of Contents

Preface vi
   DISCLAIMER viii

CHAPTER One 10
   Online Fraudster 10
   Major Terminology In Online Fraud 13
      Identity Theft /Fraud 13
      Phishing And Spoofing 14
      Spoof websites: 15
      Vishing and Smishing 17
      Data Breaches, Malware Attack. 17

Chapter Two 18
   How You Can Recognize A Potential Scam Email 18
      Spelling Error:- 18
      Grammar:- 19
      Desperation and emotional appeal:- 19
      Email address Hyperlink:- 20
      Generic emails:- 21
      Attachments:- 21
      Unknown persons:- 21
      Virus Information email:- 22
      Notices of Fine email:- 22
   Why You Need To Be Vigilant About Online Frauds ... 22

Chapter Three 26

Basic Information That You Should Know About Fraudsters......... 26

    Fraudsters are pretentious imposters:-................................. 26

    Doing quick research for authenticity:-................................. 29

    Doing financial transactions with fraudster:-....................... 32

    Fraudsters' Proposition is always juicy:-.............................. 35

    Many in One and One In Many Persons Strategy:-................ 37

Chapter Four 40

  Some Specific Strategies Of Internet Fraudsters Exposed 40

    Request For Help/Romance or Dating scam:- 41

    Business Email Compromise and suspended account:- 43

    Advance fee fraud/ Nigerian 419 Scam:-...............................45

    Fake charity Appeal for help:- 46

    Work at home job scam:-.. 46

    DDoS Attack, Ransomware and Greeting card scam:- 47

    Affinity Fraud:-... 48

    High yield investment fraud:-... 48

    Sextortion and blackmail:-... 49

    Social media / Who viewed your profile scam:- 50

    Bitcoin and Cryptocurrency frauds:- 50

    Free Wi-Fi Hotspot:-..52

    The Yahoo Boys:-...52

CHAPTER Five 54

  I Want To Be A Fraudster, Learn The Job And Stick To My Advice..54

  Personal Qualities Of A Scammer...55

- You must always think out of the Box:- 55
- Smoothtalker: 56
- Be up to date with technology and technicality:- 56
- Believability:- 57
- Research skill:- 57
- Don't be too friendly:- 57
- Develop a working plan:- 58
- Prepare your target:- 58
- Presenting your proposal:- 58
- Patience:- 58
- Don't leave a trace:- 59
- Exit Plan:- 59
- Master Scam Strategy Of The Unsung Online Fraud Heroes 60
  - The Inner Dialogue of Lazy Victims and Fraudsters 61
  - Inner Dialogue of Poor Victims and Fraudsters 62
  - FIRST STAGE 63
  - SECOND STAGE 64
  - THIRD STAGE 66

Chapter Six 67

- Me And The Scammer: My Story 67
- What To Do To An Identified Fraudster 76
- How Do You Know That You Have Been Scammed 77
- Report The Scammer 78
  - Contact other people:- 79

Talk to your Financial Institution:- 79

Contact internet crime complaint center (IC3) 79

The US Gov.'s Internet fraud website 80

eBay Security Center 80

Facebook security site 80

Chapter Seven... 82

General Precaution That Will Keep The Fraudsters Away From You 82

Preface

GREED and **IGNORANCE**..." *Exposing the unsung fraud heroes, the act of scamming, and scamming those who refuse to learn"*

The purpose of this book is to help expose the illicit act of scamming people online. The ideas presented, fortunately, will serve a dual purpose, in that it will both teach you the act of scamming to enable you to identify the scammers when you see one, and as well help those who want to learn the con-job to perfect in their tricks as some tactics employed by seasoned fraudsters has also been well documented here, for analysis.

Why would anyone want to teach people how to scam others for their hard-earned money? You might be asking. That's not the thinking of the author when he was putting this copy together; rather he had wished and still hopes that everyone should be a scammer of a sought, why using the internet. So that scam will die a natural death.

Dependable researches have shown that greed and ignorance is the main reason people get scammed on a daily bases. The logic here is that if I know what you know, you would not be able to deceive me. Of course, nobody can scam you with a trick that you already know. So the author hopes to bring the scammers and the scammed on the same page so that we would have an internet that is free of scam.

DISCLAIMER

You are solely responsible for any damage that might occur, financially or otherwise, to you as a result of applying the knowledge obtained in this book.

Ideas available in this book are based on dependable research and personal experience, gathered overtime; and provided for instructive purposes. Important facts were compiled from reliable sources to the best of the Author's knowledge.

Franklin Ndubuisi

Stay safe online

CHAPTER ONE

Online Fraudster

It's no longer news that the internet allows criminals to interact with thousands of people simultaneously. What is now the news is that people are more conscious, or even afraid of using the internet, because of the activities of fraudsters.

This illegal, ugly, and regrettable venture is as old as mankind though. Dependable researches did show that this illicit activity, although found in almost every human society, is carried out in different forms, according to social, political, and economic dynamics of the locality; and has evolved into a monster known as online Fraud.

The problem of fraudsters, scammers, tricksters, swindlers, and more recently cybercriminals, or whatever you choose to call them, is and has remained one of the major concerns of many in recent times. These Unwholesome crooks called online fraudsters, apply very clever tactics to have an undue advantage over their victims by combining old deceptive tricks with new technologies to steal peoples' money.

The advent of the internet which has made the world a global village has raised more concerns. Questions are now being asked by many who in one way or the other have fallen victims to these fraudsters on the internet. Hence we can talk of internet or web fraudsters.

A concept that became more popular with the coming of e-commerce, where fraudsters employ illegal means including but not limited to stealing of credit card information of innocent victims, in other to have access to their accounts to defraud them. Every year

Stay safe online

millions of internet users lose billions of dollars to these faceless criminals

For this book, **online** or a **web** fraudster is anyone who applies tricks on the internet, in an illegal manner to cheat others of their personal belongings, usually money and related possessions. The rate at which internet fraud is growing in recent times is not only alarming but a serious source of concern for many, regardless of your country or location; as long as you have access, and uses the internet.

"It's even more dangerous if you don't use the internet," says a financial reporter who opined that those who don't use the internet are definitely in dark about many things and as such are more prone to being a victim of bank fraud.

The growing number of victims worldwide and the sophistication of these online fraudsters is a serious source of worry for organizations, governments, and related establishments in all countries of the world. LexisNexis in their 2017 findings reported that for every dollar lost to internet fraud, organizations spend between $2.48 and $2.82 more, thereafter.

For you to avoid being scammed, you need to be informed of the various ways, tricks, actions, and inactions, as well as the requisite tools employed by fraudsters to succeed in their craft. You should also be what some has described as a smart internet consumer, to avoid the stories-that-incinerate. That is the essence of this book.

Major Terminology In Online Fraud

Identity Theft /Fraud

Anytime you see someone take somebody's details to impersonate the person's identity, such a person can be charged for identity theft. Internet Fraudsters many times steal the personal information of unsuspecting individuals without their permissions (even with their permission ignorantly though) in other to gain a certain economic or financial advantage.

Stay safe online

Information that could fall into personal data here will include Personal Residential Address, Personal phone number, Social security Number's (SSN), Passport Number, Credit Card details, and Personal Tax Information Number. Also in this category is your Pin or Password, National Insurance Number, Date of Birth, etc.

Phishing And Spoofing

This is a method used by fraudsters to trick e-mail users into disclosing their details, which the scammer needs for a fraudulent reason.

The Phisher sends a fake version of emails made to purportedly look like it came from a certain reputable company or an organization for instance, and usually; the email may have links to a pseudo website that directs would-be victims to enter their details.

They also create copycat sites, made to look like the authentic website of a real company, used primarily to obtain specified information from the would-be victims. Whether through spoofing or instant messages, the objectives are usually the same: to obtain your data.

Notable on phishing is the foremost Californian lawsuit against the teenage fraudster who created the "America Online" phishing website, which he used to defraud unsuspecting users of their personal information, and as such gained access to the money in their Bank accounts.

Spoof websites:

a scammer often creates a sub-domain site that looks like the original site with his domain name. For instance, let's say the domain name of a fraudster is Scammer.com, and he aims to steal your Payoneer fund. He creates a sub-domain: "Payoneer.scammer.com" to look exactly like "Payoneer.com". Immediately anyone enters the site and click on anything, he or she would see a pop-up requesting identity verification.

This is where you hand over, your personal information that the scammer will use to defraud you of your money because this spoof site will store your

Stay safe online

data including the login details of your Payoneer account.

Phishing is often categorized into Filter evasion, website forgery, link manipulation, and phone phishing. More often than not, the real owner of a phished mail is made to lose access to his or her mail and in many other instances they end up suffering a huge financial loss. Sometimes you're ordered to click on a particular link in an email to confirm, verify or update your bank details; with a threat to close down your account within a specified period if you fail to do as requested. Simply delete such a mail as nothing good can come out of it. In most cases, those links, attachments, etc.; may contain a virus that can harm your system

More recently the US Government has-echoed its advice for citizens to forward phishing email messages to spam@uce.gov or make a report at Federal Trade Commission (FTC). Note also that you need to get online, the name of your email services, and the arguments"full email header".

Vishing and Smishing

Vishing and smishing are also terms related to phishing when voice call and SMS texting are used by scammers: they usually demand your personal information in other to help you solve certain issues like reactivating your Credit or Debit card, update suspended account details, etc.

Data Breaches, Malware Attack.

data breaches: Data is said to have been breached when very sensitive information of an individual is entered in an unsecured environment, which may be within a corporate or an individual setting. While a **malware attack** occurs when unsafe software is designed to deactivate the computer system and make them malfunction.

Stay safe online

CHAPTER TWO

How You Can Recognize A Potential Scam Email

More than 80% of fake emails from fraudsters show at least one or two of the following characteristics that would be discussed below. Simply because they were written by inexperienced persons whose interest is just to steal your data in other to get hold of your money.

Spelling Error:-
If you read through a mail sent by a reputable organization, and that sent by a scammer, in most

cases, you will notice an obvious spelling error different from an autocorrect error. This also comes from the fact that they're always in a hurry to catch your attention. This desperation often leads to this spelling issues which should give you a clue

Grammar:-
Some of the expressions you will see in these emails are poorly structured. Sometimes, you can't but wondered if the writer ever got an elementary knowledge of English language grammar.

The reason is that they try to copy a template of an original email from the organization that they're impersonating and cut and paste some words to suit their purpose.; not bothering to see how the words correlate, thereby muzzling an appealing idea in a terrible form. You may find run-on sentences; words that are incoherently placed and poorly punctuated.

Desperation and emotional appeal:-
By now you already know that an average fraudster is desperate to have you do what he or she wants as soon as possible, so the urge to act fast is characteristic of

Stay safe online

their emails. So suspect any email that creates a certain sense of urgency. You may also see this kind of salutation: "love" "God Bless" Miss You" in some of them, depending however on the intention of the scammer, all to appeal to you, emotionally.

Most times they want you to act within a very short period, averagely 24hrs. Some are so desperate that they would ask you to act within a few minutes.

Email address Hyperlink:-
A careful check on the email addresses will reveal a very clever trick to deceive. Hence, you can find for instance a company mail address that goes thus: enquiry@franklin.com changed to enquiry@frnklin.com.

Anytime you receive a mail like this, all you need to do is to hover your cursor over the opened email header because it stores a lot of information about the email, including the source of the mail and destination, and as well as an address to reply such a mail. After which you'll see the email sender's name, which would give you an idea of whom you're dealing with. You can also do the same for the links to reveal the URL, it will amaze you to see that you're heading to www.enquiry@frnklin.com instead of www.enquiry@franklin.com

Generic emails:-

A real company will always address you by your real name as registered in their database but scammers will send you a generic email because it's usually a template kind of mail also sends to thousands of potential victims

Attachments:-

Most reputable organizations will not include an attachment in the communication of that nature: as usually done by fraudsters. This is because they know better. So, as soon as you see that call-for-action attachment, in that email, just know that a scammer is on your tail.

Unknown persons:-

Any email claim that a certain amount of money will come into your account from somebody that is not

Stay safe online

within your country is always fraudulent mail. It's as simple as that.

Virus Information email:-
Bear in mind also that any email that suggests that a certain virus has affected your personal computer is from a fraudster, as no website, for instance, is capable of having such a piece of knowledge. It's only you, the user, and the antivirus installed on your computer that can do that; to the best of my knowledge.

Notices of Fine email:-
I also learn that the FBI and related security agencies can't issue a fine to anybody online for instance; it's only a competent law court that can issue an individual or organization a fine for illegal activity on a site. So flag that email bad, that tends to suggest so.

Why You Need To Be Vigilant About Online Frauds

The rate at which internet fraudsters are penetrating cyberspace is not only worrisome but a source of concern for industry watchers. Recent researches have shown an alarming penetration of cybercriminals in almost all areas, on the internet. I came across some very worrisome recent statistical findings that I believe would interest you here.

In a very bold analysis, published by **Datafloq**, on its website, referring to "Q2 analysis of spam for 2018", it revealed that in May 2018 for instance, users of emails received more unsubscribed emails otherwise refers to as junk mail or spam than their real email messages in their mailboxes.

A study by **FirstOrion** on its own asserts that mobile phone related scam calls increased by 25% in 2018 from 2017. Again that the 3.7% mobile phone scam rate of 2017 moved up to 29.2% in 2018; adding also that the figure is expected to rise to 44% by the first quarter of 2019.

The Better Business Bureau is reported to have kept a track of internet scams in the period under review and by August 2018, it was able to register 30,263 scams

Stay safe online

It was also reported in October 2018 that Fake Advertising Applications that generate fake traffic, got over 115 million downloads. These apps are used by scammers to produce fake traffic, used to defraud advertisers of millions of dollars.

There's a total increase in the number of frauds being experienced by business organizations online. Data obtained by Experian, from its Global fraud and identity report of 2018 shows that 63% of businesses are battling more fraudulent online losses.

Norton Cybercrime report of 2013 gives us more idea of what is happening and why we should be worried. It stated that of 13,022 persons interviewed, between 18 and 64 years of age. It was learned that 49% of mobile device users use the device for work and for play, which poses more risk for mobile and e-commerce industries. Similarly, 48% of users of tablet smartphone do not observe the basic security steps like using password or security software.

Cisco in their security report of 2013 revealed that online security threats targets mostly, legitimate sites that have many users like social media platforms, consumer retail sites, and search engines; adding that adverts are 182 times likely to carry malicious content than phonographic sites. Just as an e-commerce site is 21 times more likely to give malicious content to customers than fake software, and so on.

The internet Crime Commission (IC3) in alliance with the Federal Bureau of Investigation (FBI) and the National White Collar Crime Center, in their 2007 findings as published by an online media about internet fraud, revealed that 70% of reported internet fraud was done through the 'www' sites, while 30% were carried out through emails; and of these number 44.9% reported cases of online auction Fraud, 19.0% was for non-delivered goods and services and 4.9% for check related frauds respectively.

It also adds that most of the internet frauds victims noted that they made payment through Wire transfer, Credit card, Bank debit, money order and Check, in that order.

Stay safe online

CHAPTER THREE

Basic Information That You Should Know About Fraudsters

Fraudsters are pretentious imposters:-

A Fraudster who randomly stumbles on your personal information will have difficulty relating with you. How do they solve this initial challenge? Your guess is as good as mine; they make you think that you know them somewhere, somehow.

Their first contact with you is very critical in deciding whether they would achieve their aim or not. Hence, they often pretend to be an old friend, former colleague, From a Charity organization, an old classmate, alumni associates, a government official, or even a distant family member, etc.

They can even call a few names of people you know to buttress their acquaintances to you, in other to win your trust.

Don't be deceived. If what he or she is saying is not adding up, be smart about this kind of friendly-strangers, this is the most critical part of the scam process. If you are smart at this stage you can understand the fraudster's intention and save yourself from further stress. Otherwise, you would be leading him on to the second stage where you'll hear his or her real intention, usually a juicy one.

The right thing to do is when you're not sure of who's contacting you; don't disclose more personal information about yourself. These unexpected requests can come in the form of a phone call, an email, text

Stay safe online

messages, social media chat, and many other kinds of online communication.

I can authoritatively tell you that about 95% of the scammer's deceptive proposal send at this stage, while one out of the remaining 5% that responded to the fraudster's request eventually becomes a victim.

Note also that a scammer who gets access to your ids like Driver's license or social security number can open a bank account in your name for a fraudulent purpose.

So, what do I do at this stage in other not to be rude to an old friend, who genuinely has a business proposition for me? You may ask, my advice is that you should trust nobody if you have to be impolite; it's not as bad as you may think, and you can always tender an apology. Very few people would be offended if someone says they couldn't recognize them.

The trick I use on them is to pretend that I'm very busy at the moment, with a promise to call or reply later. That's to enable me to do a random, soul searching cum personality authentication research. So when next you receive that phone call from that fellow who was so confident about how two of you wrote professional exams together some years back, think of the famous fraudster's pretentious strategy, before you respond to the request.

Doing quick research for authenticity:-
it is a known fact that fraudsters usually fake their identity. In many cases, they can impersonate a reputable person's identity, and other times they create a fictitious identity that is not verifiable online.

Now doing a quick and very thorough research will give you a very clearer perspective on whom you're dealing with. Whether as an institution, company, products, brand, names, phone number, etc. it does not matter, almost everything is searchable online. Anything you think can serve as a good keyword should be used to search before you take that step.

Now, another tricky side that I usually advise my clients is that you don't just depend on your research, as most scam websites can manipulate their way into having certain reviews that do not reflect reality.

Stay safe online

Again, they might just be new in the industry with little or nothing to learn about them; it could also be possible that you happen to be their first fraud target, and as such, you would find virtually nothing to hold on to when searching for authenticity.

Let me also warn you about the Caller ID technology, most scammers have perfected an act of faking the caller ID information; because like someone once suggested, they think they're smarter than the rest of us.

That is why you need to know that they're one step ahead of every technology. But I rather say they're one step behind every technology; the difference is the awareness level of internet users. That's why you need to be In the know.

In general, you would find very little about a smart fraudster online. So if there is very little to learn about somebody or an organization online, in this information age that everybody is competing on the internet, it is a "red flag" to ponder about.

Don't get me wrong here also as most new business organizations online would have very little presence in terms of credibility. That is why the fraudsters leverage on it, as most of them are very smart; and In fact, the 21st-century internet scammer knows what to do to succeed daily, in other not to go out of business.

Though very many scammers still bank on the ignorant of many to continue to defraud people even with an already blacklisted strategy, others are very innovative in their ideas and mode of operation.

What else can I do if cannot trust the information I get from online research? Talk to somebody. Yes! I like to tell my clients to always confide in someone, especially if they think the person is an authority in the area that they might need help. The same thing should be applied here.

Before you give that information or agree to that request from that person that you're not sure of his or her trustworthiness, tell a friend. The person you're confiding in might be in the right frame of mind to give

Stay safe online

useful advice, even if such a person is not an expert: a good Telepathy comes in handy here.

Doing financial transactions with fraudster:-

One funny thing that fraudsters do that baffles me is when they make their victims do something on trust, especially when it involves finances. How on earth will I agree to make an upfront payment for something I'm not sure of its value, to someone else, just because he or she said it's the right thing to do. I have heard funny stories of how people make an upfront payment to a loan offers by fraudsters, sometimes is for a promise of a job offer.

Others may require that you pay money to redeem a prize that they said you've won. The more interesting part is that they're not ready to trust you in return just in case you want them to do the opposite of what they're requesting. That's why they even threaten to deny you whatever it is, they're offering you if you're not willing to cooperate with them. No wonder, they're always in a hurry to make you part with your money.

Let me also add that even if you have to pay money to somebody that you don't have access to or that the person has requested that you pay the money through a particular method of payment. You need to consider the safest means of payment that protects you, in case something goes wrong. That is why credit card payment is still the best when compared to wiring money through MoneyGram or Western Union for example; because it's not very easy to get your money back using the latter. So you should be at alert when that your supposed genuine business partner asks to be paid through certain means of payment.

By now you should know that Banks take days to release funds deposited through Checks. Be sure that a Check is confirmed by your bank before releasing those goods, or even wire money to that customer who may turn out to be a scammer that gave you a fake Check.

If you think you're prone to financial attack by fraudsters, do well to sign up for scam alerts with your local law enforcement authorities, to be abreast with the latest tricks employed by fraudsters.

Stay safe online

Buying things online could be very tricky with the high rate of Scam sites available on the internet. You already know that scammers thrive on fake identities. So before you begin to enter your details on any website, use all the available security measures to confirm the authenticity of the company. If you have to, you should confirm the address, phone number, etc. the rule, however, is to stick to trusted sites.

Any secure payment site that is independently confirmed to be secured will have a padlock symbol, followed by the "HTTPS" letters at the beginning of the web address. What this means is that any sensitive personal information entered on these encrypted sites will be protected from any interception by unauthorized parties.

A scary side to these secure sites issue is that many phishing sites also have the "HTTPS" attached. So do remember to check if the real name of the company is included in the URL.

This would serve as a hint on whether the site is been run by the company or a fraudster. Do also remember that it's not all the websites that employ the technicality that could make their name display, in their URL address. But doing this smart check with the right intuition you're very unlikely to enter the wrong site.

Fraudsters' Proposition is always juicy:-

When an idea, suggestion, or proposition appear too real to be true, you need to give it a second thought. Why would anyone want to declare you the winner of a lottery that you did not enter for, or offer you a job that you never apply for? If you're very emotional about it, little research may be all that is needed to escape their trap.

I will share my personal experience a few years back; after obtaining my first degree in mass communication, I was in desperate need of a job.

That fateful day, a friend told me to call a guy who he said is the personnel manager of a reputable firm in my neighborhood, who informed him of a job opening in the company. I put a call across to the guy, he told me that he was ready to offer me the job if I can give

Stay safe online

him $200 worth of cash. According to this crook, the monthly payment for the job is about $1500.

I was honestly interested, and so I asked for the specifics of the job. He gave a detailed analysis and requirements. I told him that I was not sure I could pass the interview as I couldn't meet a certain requirement.

He said that notwithstanding, as long as I could afford his fee of $200, he would give me the job. My friend whom I later learned is a partner in the crime had urged me to pay the money before someone else does; as such a job racket is rampant in my country.

I did a little search on the company and came up with a memo recently circulated by the company to its staff suggesting that the company is shutting down operations in the city and laying off staff because of insecurity in the region.

I told my friend of my findings, he pretended to be ignorant. But unfortunately, two order persons are already victim to the same job scam by this crook of a friend; as I was told.

Many in One and One In Many Persons Strategy:-

Another important thing you need to know about scammers is the fact that one person can pull a deal with you. In some cases, it's two or more persons working together. You could also fall victim to a scammer who operates as multiple individuals trying to get at you in different forms hoping that one of his or her personality will catch your interest.

This occurs when a particular scammer poses as a travel representative when that fails he tries to contact you again as a solicitor. Another time he is a Bank Manager, Traditional ruler, or even a government official, and so on.

Again, you can meet a ring of scammers that not only work as a team but have perfected the act in such a way that each person can communicate with you from a different location but in a manner that would make you think that you're talking with the same person.

Stay safe online

These scammers are very skillful and these categories of fraudsters are the ones I refer to as "Professional fraudsters"

It's pretty difficult to escape from their trap, or even arresting them; because as you already know, their names are usually fake or stolen, and their contact phone numbers and addresses, more often are clones or registered with fake information. And so, doing a name or phone number search, might not help in some circumstances.

Though, doing a reverse image search on their photos can give you something to work on. That too is not 100% as I learned recently. If a particular image appears with different names or as a stock image on a site, it should be a red flag.

Note also that scammers do pass your personal information to other fraudsters who in turn will try to scam you with a different tactic. And because they lack morals, scammers will want to scam you again and again. Guess what? Once they see that you're vulnerable, they capitalize on your ignorance to milk you dry. So before we say, Jack Robinson, flee from that fraudster.

Stay safe online

CHAPTER FOUR

Some Specific Strategies Of Internet Fraudsters Exposed

It's worthy of note to say here that a scammer may be a citizen of any country, state, or province. Sometimes they're from a city different from your location. You might also be in the same city as them.

They can even be a resident or your next-door neighbor or still, a friend, and in specific cases a family member. That is how deadly they are. But our concern here is that they've flooded our internet, and because of the wide reach of the internet, that scammer can operate from any location.

Below are some of their strategies:

Request For Help/Romance or Dating scam:-

You have just received a mail from that your very rich social media friend requesting help. Both of you have been communicating for some time now. He or she has been sending very sweet romantic messages to you. And has also professed love to you, and wishes to meet you as soon as he or she can.

He or she can go as far as making a marriage proposal. And you begin to give him or her requisite attention, thinking that he or she is into you for real. Suddenly this ruthless scammer who said he or she is a citizen of a certain country, for instance, Being affected by dreadful currency devaluation, sends you a message; requesting for a transfer of a certain amount of his or her money to your bank account to avoid further depreciation of the currency value.

Stay safe online

This fellow would agree to give you a cut of the wealth. How do I help you? You're already asking in your mind. Now he or she needs access to your Bank account in other to facilitate the transfer.

You send him your account details, including a "small fee" for the wire transfer expenses. Your rich lover swiftly empties your life savings.

This mind-blowing trick has made and continued to make many scammers rich. No wonder there is an ever-growing list of fake online dating profiles of them. And for every one busted fraudster, there are hundreds of them more lurking behind; hoping to catch susceptible people that are ready to give away their personal information and money for love and relationship.

According to an online report quoting the British Journal of Criminology recently, the psychological method used by fraudsters in online dating fraud is the same as that of domestic violence issues.

Business Email Compromise and suspended account:-

Fraudsters work so hard to hack or steal company emails and use the same to defraud the company. These scammers who are sometimes the staff of the company, former staff, or someone who has a mule in the company, are well connected to highly placed individuals in the system. This trick has diverse variation, and mostly targeted at new employees in the financial department; usually those in charge of payment.

This is because the new staff sometimes does not know much about the internal working of the system yet, and are under pressure to impress their Boss.

The scammer succeeds in gaining access to the company's email password and he wants to get some cash from the company. He sends you an urgent email requesting an immediate wire transfer of a certain amount of money to a foreign account. Let's say a US bank account if the company is located in West Africa for instance.

Stay safe online

The purpose of the transfer payment may be to offset a bill owed to a foreign partner or anything of a similar nature. The scammer is already aware of the communication channel of your company, and you happen to be the one in charge of payment on behalf of the company.

You did not bother to confirm this message through a different communication channel. Now the money goes into this US Bank account set up for this purpose by either the scammer's foreign partner or an unsuspecting person who genuinely wanted to help a friend. The fraudster withdraws the money from where ever he or she is operating. The rest of the story becomes history.

They can use that email to contact customers of the company and make them reveal sensitive company information. Or still, they can create a copycat email, and use it to send messages to customers of the company (Financial Institutions), telling them that their account has been suspended; and requesting them to update personal information in a redirected phishing websites in other to harvest victim's data.

Advance fee fraud/ Nigerian 419 Scam:-

The advance fee fraud comes in so many forms but the key thing here is that you're always requested to part with a certain amount of money, to have them render a certain service to you. Such services are usually too good to be true. The scammer is also aware of that and as such in a hurry to have you accede to their request before anyone else hears about it.

The trick could range from a job offer in which you're required to pay a processing fee, a lottery that you'd won, a certain individual making you a beneficiary of their wealth, etc. Closely related to this is the Nigerian 419 scam. It's so-called because of its origin. Fraudsters send an email to you asking you to help certain government officials move embezzled money from the country to a US bank account for instance, with a promise of a handsome reward. Of course, the deal requires an upfront charge that you have to offset. This is where they catch you.

Stay safe online

Section 419 of the Nigerian penal code stipulates punishment for this offense, which incidentally is where it derives its name from. The country's local financial crime commission EFCC is seriously fighting the menace.

Fake charity Appeal for help:-
Fraudsters create fake charity organizations and try to use them to defraud well-meaning individuals who are willing to help those in need through charity donation. More often you get an email requesting help for certain flood victims, displaced persons in need of relief materials, etc. You log in to their fake website and transfer money to them. LOL! You have just thrown your money to the wind and most times have also given them your credit card details for related fraudulent activities.

Work at home job scam:-
This one includes both fake job offers that require an upfront payment and scam artists on the internet parading as online marketers. They usually show you fake evidence of how they're making one million dollars in a week for instance and try to buttress their

point with Photoshop-screenshots of their purported financial statements. Those who fall victim to this trap subscribe to either their useless training or those copy and paste eBooks that would not help you in any way.

They usually downplay the essence of hard work to make you believe that you can be sleeping all day while your money works for you, even when they cannot offset their bills, despite having such a wealth of knowledge.

DDoS Attack, Ransomware and Greeting card scam:-

They can send you what seems like an e-card from a friend or family member that is infected by malware. Clicking on it would have the virus transferred automatically to your system. Ransomware is a malware spell that uselessly encrypts your files, and of course, the attacker will require money from you for a decrypt. And if it's a DDoS attack, the fraudster can shut down your site and make you lose access; even internet service providers are not free from this as a web-server hosting a site, for instance, are drowned with traffic that usually overpowers them; making DDoS Attack a very serious online threat.

Affinity Fraud:-
Fraudsters capitalize on common interest, usually of belief (religion) to make you part with your money- especially within an online religious community. A lot of people feel comfortable dealing with those with common religious affiliation, and fraudsters are aware of this; hence they capitalize on it to defraud followers of their money.

These fraudsters mostly claim to have been mandated by some form of divinity. and because of religious inclination ignorant followers are lured into an unwholesome investment that they end up losing their money.

High yield investment fraud:-
Fraudsters create a lot of programs that promise high investment interest. In this category are all those Ponzi and pyramid schemes that provide wide and unrealistic dreams of how you can double the value of your investment within a short time etc. most of these

ill-fated business organizations and investment schemes usually do not have a tangible product that they offer.

They rather depend on new members to settle earlier investors. Very many of this kind of investment is in their number online, hoping to cash in on greedy fellows, and majorly ignorant investors.

Sextortion and blackmail:-
People's private nude images are used to get money from them.

Those who finally became victims of this were not aware of what their partner was planning as at the time they were handing in their nude to them. You might have a video call with your friend who requested that both of you should go naked. You thought it was just fun until you get a video clip of that, from that friend threatening to make a mess of your personality online; unless you settle him with some cash.

Stay safe online

Social media / Who viewed your profile scam:-

Scammers know that people develop curiosity in this area, especially Facebook users, hence, they put up a pop-up that asks you to download an app that would enable you to see who's viewed your profile. This is another way they employ to gain access to your account including login details.

They can even start using it to ask your friends for money as if you're the one doing the asking. They can create a false news headline or anything that can catch your interest. Once you click on it, you're asked to log in with your social media account. Just know that you're handing over your account to fraudsters. A scammer can also create a duplicate account of a friend and send you a request, just to have access to your personal information.

Bitcoin and Cryptocurrency frauds:-

The advent of Bitcoin and many other coins in the Crypto-currency market has made it a fraudster's heaven-majorly because of anonymity in its transactions. Scams here ranges from fake coin exchange platform, where only the "Buy button" will be available: those who buy cannot sell; to hacking the platform, to make investors lose their money. Another scam here, though more like a strategy is "Pump and dump".

A term used by crypto investors to describe an arranged buying of a particular coin, usually an unknown coin to cause sudden price rise that will attract genuine investors who will, in turn, watch their investment depreciate when those who initiated the idea to pump the coin, sell off theirs, at a specified date. Other forms of fraud-related activities in Cryptocurrency include fake cloud mining companies, mining, and ICO Exit scam.

The Initial coin Offering (ICO) of a worthless coin by scammers is done to harvest the investment capital of investors, after which the website used for such purpose goes under and scammers disappear with the investor's fund.

Stay safe online

Free Wi-Fi Hotspot:-

A scammer can set up a free Wi-Fi connection in a public place hoping to catch lovers of free connection. If you login to the free connection, your computer is already hacked as the scammer will have access to your data on the computer. To avoid this, always ensure that your computer does not connect automatically to an open Wi-Fi network by turning off the option in your computer Wi-Fi setting.

The Yahoo Boys:-

These are a special group of online scammers that operates with different tactics. They do not have any specific area of operation or a particular strategy but are more deadly than any other group of fraudsters that have been discussed so far.

The name Yahoo is attached to their name simply because the originators of the scamming scheme from a West African country called Nigeria are alleged to have started it with their Yahoo emails. The earliest Yahoo boys were mainly focused on advance fee fraud, dating scams, and the likes. But the present-day yahoo boys have gone cosmic, with many consulting local spiritualist and magicians to enhance their "trade".

A quick search online would reveal how they have been accused by locals of stealing female undies, for ritual purposes. This is because they not only tell stories to their victims to trick them into paying money to them, they try hypnotizing them.

Other areas that you can be scammed including insurance, health, elder/seniors, grandparent and grandchild's, tax, prize, Technical support, travel, fake refund, etc. The list is endless. All that is required is instinct and vigilance.

CHAPTER FIVE

I Want To Be A Fraudster, Learn The Job And Stick To My Advice

But before you jump to scamming people listen to the word on the marble: the holy book says, "God can't be deceived. Whatsoever anyone does, he or she must surely get the reward."

Franklin Ndubuisi

Personal Qualities Of A Scammer

Learning the act of scamming people is not an easy job, like every other occupation, those who I refer to as "Professional fraudsters" are people that can be associated with certain kind of personal traits which fortunately or unfortunately helps them to succeed in the "game".

So in case, you have been trying to scam people in the past without any success, just know that you need to perfect your skill by adhering to the following qualities that have distinguished the famous "Nigerian prince" fraudsters and many others.

Why am I teaching people to be a scammer? Remember, the sole aim of this book is to make everyone on the globe a potential scammer in such a way as to make scamming die a natural death.

You must always think out of the Box:-
Yes, the keyword here is creativity. You must think of a new way, a new angle, and a new story that would be different from that which is already known in the

Stay safe online

public domain. Otherwise, you'll be sweating your ugly ass off the internet all day long without any achievement. And the worst part of being a serial scam failure is that you're constantly exposing yourself to the security agencies that are constantly monitoring you and your guys; hoping that you fall into their net soon.

Smoothtalker:
Have you heard of "Mr. Charming" before? Well, he does not exist anywhere on earth. But he's been created daily in the Romantic world by the smooth talker. They make their women see them as Mr. charming of their dream. For you to successfully scam people at this information age, you should be able to, as they say, "build a castle in the air", in the minds of your target victims; especially if your "scam office" is on dating sites.

Be up to date with technology and technicality:-
You have to be in the know of the latest technology, policies and the likes so that you'll be abreast with the right information. Otherwise, you would be walking yourself into the trap of security agencies; especially if

you depend much on technology to get information from people.

Believability:-
Your stories and ideas must be that which creates a true reflection of reality unless you want to be an object of ridicule on the "job".

Research skill:-
You must know how to do a comprehensive check on people's personal life and achievements so that you can follow up appropriately. Research to know what your target likes, dislikes, things that motivate them, hopes and aspirations, etc. with the sole aim of manipulating them to get a result.

Don't be too friendly:-
While it's advised that you establish a cordial relationship with your target in certain circumstances that require such, you must not be too friendly. Remember, you're offering a "too good to be true" opportunity. Being too friendly will speed up suspicion.

Stay safe online

Develop a working plan:-
Scamming is an unscrupulous venture that required a systematic approach. If a format is not working, you may try another. You must have an idea of what to do when to start a process and the right time to end it. You should also know when a strategy is working or not, and as well as when to apply the exit plan.

Prepare your target:-
You don't rush into the deal, you need to sizzle of your target and groom them to the climax. This is a process of trust-building to make them lose their guard for you to strike.

Presenting your proposal:-
Be sure that you have studied enough about your target; you have known their strength and weakness before you let the cat out of the bag.

Patience:-
Being patient with your target is not only a virtue on this "job" but a tool that you need at any point in time to succeed. I know that you as a scammer is desperate and always in a hurry to make them pay. You should

not neglect the importance of patience in your desperation.

Don't leave a trace:-
All your effort in making that rich fellow transfer thousands of dollars into your account will come to nothing if you leave a trail that will give you away. So if you want to come-clean in all your deals, always ensure that there's no loose end.

One of the important tools you need to do that is in hiding your IP address. Always use a convenient financial institution to cash out your loot. Ensure that your grammar is in other in all your communication, if possible use grammar checking software so that you can pull through those special deals.

Exit Plan:-
Exit when you think, there's nothing more to work on, or when you sense a complication that can be life-threatening. Remember, as a hero, you must be live to fight again, otherwise, you'll become history.

Stay safe online

Master Scam Strategy Of The Unsung Online Fraud Heroes

The reason why we feel that our day-to-day efforts are not worth the trouble, compared to what we go true daily is that we have an "alternative". A utopian alternative created by those I call "intelligent" idiots who parade themselves as online experts.

Although these persons intelligently create an alternative for us, and we not only buy into these factitive alternatives, we also pretend that these alternatives are what we are enjoying rather than reality.

To say the obvious everybody hates being poor if at all there's anything like being poor. Everybody wants to be rich. These intelligent sets of people know what we want, and they think that our stupidity should be of benefit to them at all cost.

Unfortunately, this same subtle group of scammers is often celebrated by their victims with a name that has been popularized as "online gurus". Did I hear you say, online gurus? I call them "the unsung online fraud heroes" Now put on your thinking cap as I show you what these unsung fraud heroes do to your mindset that makes them succeed.

The Inner Dialogue of Lazy Victims and Fraudsters

Lazy Victims: "To make money online is very easy; we can even be sleeping why the internet is making money for us. We need to start getting passive income that doesn't require effort and enjoy better life like others."

Fraudsters: "Yes! You're right. You can do it like us, don't you know that we make free money every day on the internet, your effort is not required and 100% instant success is guaranteed."

You're deceived by these seductive words, and they position themselves as masters to milk you dry.

Fraudsters: "We need to make these idiots believe that we make free money on the internet. We need to show them photographs of how successful our life is.

Stay safe online

How we can travel to any part of the world, by flying only on business class seats, unless we want to go with our private jets. Again, Show them images of our vacations in which we often get handshakes with personalities like the US President. We'll also send to them screenshots of our doctored accounts statement where we earn more than $10,000 daily.

"Yes! We'll show them images of those state-of-the-art tourist sites that we've visited, and make them believe we live such a lifestyle every day."

At this point you're already salivating on how you will join the league of millionaires, having met the much-awaited messiah. IMAO!

Inner Dialogue of Poor Victims and Fraudsters

PoorVictims: "how long are we going to remain in this life of hardship? Life is unfair to us, we deserve something better in life."

Fraudsters: "Everyone can be rich including you; as long as you want to and meet the right people. Don't you know that you can choose the kind of life you want? Poverty and riches are in your hand if only you believe. Let me tell you the secret of my success: I'm a giver. You must be a generous giver because 'givers never lack'. Don't be afraid to transfer your life savings to our accounts, it's the will of the invisible spirit and act of divinity that will make you be like us."

Their messages of hope brainwash you and you begin to live like a dreamer while contributing daily for their upkeep. LOL!

FIRST STAGE
Victims: "What kind of business is this? We've spent thousands of our hard-earned money with nothing to show for it. The worst part is that, rather than sleeping all night as we were told, we now stay awake all night, monitoring our investment. It's either this business is not as easy as we were told or there's something they're not telling us."

Fraudsters: "You children of little faith, how can you quit so easily. Have you not hear that 'failing is the first step to succeeding?' this is why we did not tell you everything about this business because we have a

Stay safe online

feeling that you're comfortable in your 'comfort zone' that's why you're complaining of failure. An ordinary failure? In business, you must fail many times, but you don't have to lose focus on your target."

As honest as their advice will seem to you, there's always a hidden agenda. You're now a step away from reality if you're wise, you'd run away from the fraudster otherwise you'll enter stage two.

SECOND STAGE
Victims: "So what do we do now? We need to beg these online business experts to teach us more about how they truly became successful."

Fraudsters: "Hard work cannot make you rich, a simple strategy is what you need. We know what you need but unfortunately, we're very busy with our business. We don't even have time for leisure, so one on one coaching will be very expensive, it's only for those that can afford it. But, because we want every one of you to succeed like us, we'll send you our eBooks that will cost you a little money compared to your take-home from the business.

"You can also follow us on our Twitter handle, Facebook pages, Instagram or study our profile on LinkedIn, visit our blogs to read recent advice. We'll also Pin some learning strategies on Pinterest so that you can ask your questions in Quora. Be assured that we'll reply to you through your email.

"Those of you who cannot afford to pay for our eBooks should forget about making money online; because 'anything that costs nothing is worth nothing'. Hurry and order a copy of the eBooks as soon as possible because we have limited copies. Like we keep telling our students, what we are offering you is a lifetime opportunity. Your life will be miserable if you keep working for somebody all your life. It's time to be your boss."

And these words, activate a panic button in your ignorant mindset; you want to be the first to order their eBooks before everyone else does. And their account balances increase while yours further depreciates.

Stay safe online

THIRD STAGE

Some of you, haven't purchased these Books would have realized that it contains mostly, what you already know. What trash! But the rest are too dumb to decipher, and as such will follow the fraudster to the third stage.

Victims: "This whole thing sounds interesting but is very technical. Some of us have applied some of the strategies that they listed here, but we're still not making it like these 'internet gurus'"

Fraudsters: "The keyword here now is patience. 'Patience is a virtue 'that's all you need now. That's what every entrepreneur should know. But for those that are still not clear about how they would succeed, you can also request the Audio version of our success strategy. It will show you in practice, how we turned those strategies to wealth. We sincerely believe that it would add to your knowledge."

This is the exit stage, at this stage, they have succeeded in selling their trash of ideas to you, and you're now left in your wilderness of thought.LOL!

CHAPTER SIX

Me And The Scammer: My Story

As a city journalist of many years, it would be ironic for me to say that experience is not the best teacher, contrary to an elementary understanding of a saying that experience is the best teacher. Experience with the fraudsters will teach you more than you need to know.

But it's one that anyone would want to have. That's how I feel when I set out to investigate the activities of the internet fraudsters. I needed to have a first-hand kind of knowledge of their recent strategies.

Stay safe online

I wanted a story I'll tell my readers. Are you thinking what I'm thinking? Don't get me wrong on this, because I honestly didn't subscribe to losing money on the internet, so that I will come here to attract sympathy by telling you how I lost money to a certain fraudster. Nobody will want to lose hard-earned money just to have a story for his readers

That notwithstanding, I wanted something much more than losing money. What on earth would that be? You're asking already.

Well, you know that sudden subtle mix of excitement that you get as a young man, when that older pretty female that you have a crush on, met you randomly and tells you that she's in love with you. While you're still trying to figure out her real intention for saying what she'd said, you got a very passionate invitation to dinner.

On arrival, you discovered that this seductive lady is ready to have you on her already arranged seduction bed. You find your heart trapped between your desires to satisfy an undeniable urge without being caught and your moral dignity, which is about to be stolen.

That is the kind of feeling I wanted with these fraudsters. So I wanted to be scammed or what? Not sure what it was anyway, but I knew I needed something very secretive and pleasurable.

The next was where to locate the scammers. I know that millions of them are out there on every segment on the internet, but I wanted I place where I could immediately hook up with one.

At first, I didn't know exactly where to start from; but as believed by a school of thought that you need to be a thief, to catch a thief, I needed to be a scammer also in other to catch the scammer. Thoughts flickered through my mind before I decided to begin with the dating sites. So now I would be sitting on a chair with my laptop communicating with a certain idiot who does not give a dime about my well-being?

Unfortunately, I had little knowledge of how the dating websites run, as, over my 12 years of being active on

Stay safe online

the internet, I have never registered on any dating site. At various times in the past, while working on a certain serious project, I have had that annoying pop-up advert urging me to click here to chat with so and so persons. I had ignored those attractive images like a plague until now.

So this is how I began the missionary journey with a very popular dating site, whose name I will not mention here for an obvious reason. It took about an hour or so to set up my already prepared pseudo scammer's profile. I created two different profiles, one for a female and another for a male. The only genuine data that I had on that platform was my mobile phone number.

The male profile had an image of my late father, while that of a female had an image of a close relative who died recently in a ghastly car accident. Both pictures were taken from my stock of picture collection, which I had snapped at different times as a photojournalist.

So that the scammers will think that I'm real when they do an image search about any of them. One good thing about that of my late father's is that I still manage his Facebook page that gives it sought of credibility.

After filling in those boring questions and suggestions that are synonymous with dating sites, I was now ready to start the hunting. Two days dragged by with no single response from anyone. I was rather anxious for a hook-up but I was not willing to contact anyone for that purpose because my aim was not to establish any relationship but to understand the ways of the dating fraudsters.

I was also aware that there are thousands of genuine love-seekers on that platform. It seems attractively difficult differentiating who is a scammer from genuine ones, I later learned; as almost all the people that I viewed and researched on their profiles seem genuine.

It seems these con artists have top up their game, I was thinking. Or was I rushing the whole racket? I had paused for a moment to ponder. If there is anything I didn't know that it's a job that requires patience. Few persons that I later stumbled on randomly as the day

Stay safe online

progresses did not give me a clue of what I was looking for. I felt perhaps the scammers have detected that I'm a fellow scammer of sought and has decided to avoid me.

It was not until I got a message on my male profile page from a young female, supposedly a teen who later told me that she turned 18yrs a month ago and was willing to hit the road with me.

I honestly did not want to engage in any kind of discussion with this "little angel" as I tagged her, because I could not find anything incriminating about her, online. She has a scanty online presence, corroborating her profile story that her aunt whom she grew up with restricted her from using social media, until now. But when I saw that she was in the same city as me, I felt perhaps I could just have a fun time with her. However, I was wrong.

We chatted about ten times in five days before I developed a second thought about her. She suddenly went offline. We couldn't talk for two days before I got a phone call from an unknown number (a female) asking to speak to Mr. Ahaotu(my late father). Of course, I knew immediately who it was.

She introduced herself and narrated how her aunt caught her in a late-night chat with a friend, and in a resultant scuffle, her laptop was damaged. That was why she had been offline. I told her I was sorry for her ordeal, as she suggests that I could reach her with the said number anytime I want to.

The next day I saw her online, we got talking as usual; she was saying something like needing money to buy some stuff. I said to myself, this lady has pressed the panic button, so I have to be smart with her so that I don't come here to tell my readers how I was outsmarted by this "little rat" who was possibly working with a guy at the background.

I told her that I'm still depending on my pension and a little royalty from an investment for now, and as such could not afford extra cash for her.

Stay safe online

Fraudsters are very smart people. They must have guessed that the initial tactics could not work on me, and had decided to try another option.

She called me on the phone a day after asking if I'll be interested in working for a certain offshore oil servicing firm, she could help me secure a job in the company; adding that she has a job slot in the company as part of her shareholding benefits that she inherited from her father.

I told her that it'll be fine if she can. She said she had already spoken to the managing director who will schedule a formal interview and subsequently, an employment letter. She also said she's using a cropped copy of my profile photo to get a temporary permit card that will give me access to the MD. I just said ok, not knowing exactly what to say as the line went dead.

That night I was doing serious thinking about what was going on. A job just like that, I had an urge to call her back and tell her not to proceed with what she was doing but instinct told me not to.

Franklin Ndubuisi

Two days later I got a strange call from a man who addressed me as an accomplice to a forgery case against one Miss Jennifer that is being interrogated for being in possession of a forged company private document that has my initials. After which he asked if I was willing to offset the $200 worth of fine or have both of us charged and possibly sentenced to six months in prison.

I simply cut the connection because I didn't know exactly what to say. I felt a momentary surge of disgust for being judged as an accomplice. Of what exactly! I tried to imagine.

If not for the fake information in their possession, these idiots would have gotten me with this threat to tarnish my reputation. I began to think about the extent to which fraudsters go just to defraud people in my country.

In case you still want to know how it ended, I simply ignored them, and up till today, nothing was heard of this Jennifer of a girl and her man. I had to exit the dating site without any notice.

Stay safe online

What To Do To An Identified Fraudster

Avoid meeting them in person because they can be very dangerous with little or no remorse for their actions. We have all heard stories of people thoroughly beaten and sometimes murdered by these internet fraudsters when they met face-to-face with fraudsters.

Stop all forms of communication with them immediately. Block them in your social media pages if you're already connected with them and delete all sweet chat that evokes good memories about them, nothing good can come from them.

Flag their emails as spam, give their websites bad reviews and flag their phone numbers and bank account details, blacklist their photos as scammers, etc.

If you have enough evidence that you think can incriminate them, please do report them to the appropriate authority before they scam your friends.

Recover your Identity from the scammer: at any point that you notice an identity theft issue on your identity, never hesitate to start a process of recovering it, to avoid more damage in the near future. Among the things you could do in this regard includes contacting iDCare: learn more of how this works at the iDcare website. You can also request for Commonwealth Victims certificate: it will assist your claim of being a victim of identity theft.

How Do You Know That You Have Been Scammed

1. If something you paid for online was not delivered to you and you can't trace it.

2. If the person who bought your goods online has disappeared without paying for the goods

3. If what was received was not exactly the description of what was advertised.

Stay safe online

4. If someone said that a particular investment is 100% guaranteed and you still lose your capital rather than make a profit.

5. If they have sold an idea to you that all you need to do to be financially free is to become an internet guru, and you're paying through your nose trying to learn every package and programs online.

Report The Scammer

Now that you have been defrauded, you need not be ashamed of it nor allow the scammer to continue in his or her illicit business. Expose the scam and the scammer by reporting the incident to the appropriate authority. There are so many such agencies. Your location should not be an issue, just as some can scam you online from any region of the world; he or she can also be tracked and arrested from any region. So be smart to be equipped with relevant information.

Contact other people:-
Once you confirm that a particular individual or an organization is a fraudster, the first thing to do is to contact your friends, family members, or even the public to warn them to beware of such an individual or organization, if possible describe the tactics been used to people so that they would not fall prey to any scammer using such tactics.

Talk to your Financial Institution:-
Especially if the fraud is related to banking transactions, credit card issues, online purchases, sharing of personal information with a scammer, loss of sensitive documents, etc. that could put you at risk of more loss.

Contact internet crime complaint center (IC3)
They're in partnership with the Federal Bureau of investigations (FBI)and the National White Collar crime center. You can always report to any of them. This is where you report hacking, online extortion, identity theft, and many other cybercrimes.

Stay safe online

There's also the **Online Better Business Bureau of the US and Canada,** which has a website that aids consumer's complaints against e-commerce and other online businesses. By also searching her database, you can determine if there are related complaints against the same organization and the current status of the complaint.

The US Gov.'s Internet fraud website
This is another fast way of reporting that online fraud.

There's also **the Craigslist fraud prevention page**, dedicated to fraud-related complaints. You will find more useful information on her "avoiding Scam" page.

eBay Security Center
This is a very useful place to report marketplace fraud especially online auction-related frauds.

Facebook security site
This helps you in case your account is hacked etc.

But before you take any step, gather your facts: internet auction, for instance, you need to know the name of the seller, item sold, seller's username, address, date, and time of close of the sale. You can also report to the auction host: with a dispute or mediation services, it might be resolved.

Stay safe online

CHAPTER SEVEN

General Precaution That Will Keep The Fraudsters Away From You

You must not communicate to anybody of your Personal Bank PINs, as even Banks will never request such on the phone or through email.

- Contact your Bank immediately you notice any unusual activity in your account.
- As a rule, Public Wi-Fi is not always secure, including some hotspots
- As a seller, always confirm payment before releasing your goods

- Prefer Credit Card and secure payment services over Debit Cards
- Secure your password, writing it on paper, or storing it on the computer is a poor way of securing it. Memorizing from the head is the surest
- Always patronize reliable financial institutions when doing any money transfer.
- After paying online, always re-check your Bank Statement details.
- It's not always a good idea to receive the fund on behalf of somebody.
- Find time to read the site's privacy and return policy before making a payment on the platform.
- For reference keep safe, a copy of your order and payment acknowledgment received.
- You must update your computer software, your browsers, and relevant applications where necessary.
- Personally educate yourself, your kids, friends, and family members on how to be responsible

Stay safe online

online, as regard to the risk involved in doing any form of communication with a stranger.

- If you use a personal laptop, ensure that it's protected from unwanted access.
- Try changing your online password occasionally.
- Always subscribe to two-factor authentication in any platform to be sure of any transaction.
- It not advisable to click on email links or attachments that you're not sure of the source
- It's not advisable to use a single password for multiple accounts.
- Consider turning off your device once it's not in use to make it less prone to spyware attacks.
- Any website that begins with "HTTP" is not encrypted, hence are not secure, always look for the "HTTPS" sites: encrypted sites
- Always do a Reverse image search on personal photos of your internet contacts whose identity you're not sure of
- Suspect every internet stranger who is eager to meet with you for any reason.

- If that stranger claims to be residing in the US for example, doing a background check on him or she would save you thousands of Dollars
- Report lost Credit or Debit card Immediately
- Beware of those around you while you're using ATM or making online financial transactions.
- Watch out for skimmers- tricky devices that could harvest your details at an ATM spot. These skimmers in their nature can be installed and uninstalled in seconds. So be vigilant.
- Always go with your print out the receipt from the ATM. Don't just throw it away carelessly, you never know who's monitoring you as those print out could be used to get your account information.
- Anything that contains your account information like old checks, sensitive documents should be properly destroyed; you'll not know who will get hold of it.
- Always write your checks in permanent blue ink, it makes it harder for alteration and never leaves a blank space

Stay safe online

- Written checks should not be seen through envelopes and sent through a secure mailbox.
- Never send money to anyone you met on the internet unless you're sure who they are.
- Do not open suspicious pop-up windows links or attachments that you're not sure of. Float completely on links to see where it lead
- Do not respond to any call request about your computer remote access.
- Put very little information about you on your social media page
- Remember to install a pop-up blocker on your device
- Make sure you subscribe to email and text transaction alerts for your Bank accounts
- Don't leave your card on a system unattended.
- Make sure you know the meaning of all pre-checked boxes before you order online.

www.ingramcontent.com/pod-product-compliance
Lightning Source LLC
Chambersburg PA
CBHW070301220526
45465CB00004B/1696